CLEAR LEADERSHIP:

Five powerful and proven skills to maximize your leadership influence

Table of Contents

Introduction: The Art of Influence

"Leadership is the art of getting someone else to do something you want done because he wants to do it."

-Dwight D. Eisenhower

So, what is Leadership, anyway?

Leadership is the art of influencing others. Influence is acquired from the people who have chosen to willing follow you. In order to start acquiring influence with another person you need to bond with them and form a relationship.

Eisenhower's quote neatly lays out that the best method to get things accomplished is to influence other people in such a way that they *want* to carry out the mission of their leader. Please take note of the big difference between **want to** and **have to**. Titles and authority only offer face value compliance whereas influence and persuasion will achieve buy in and commitment.

Traditional leadership circles believe that to keep a contrived distance from their employees is important to project a certain kind of image of confidence, competence, control and authority. The twisted irony about this kind of thinking is that it stifles and hinders connection – the very thing you need in order to build influence with other people.

Let's face a quick fact, people don't quit their company, they quit their boss. Employees don't and cannot have real loyalty to their companies;

they have loyalty to the people in them. Employees associate all their opinions, thoughts and emotions about their job based almost entirely on how they are treated at work by their boss(es). Much like how customers base their opinions, thoughts and feelings and how they are treated by the employees they interact with.

It shouldn't be too hard to see that if leadership teams fail to build real and honest relationships with their teams, nothing will really ever change with regards to employee engagement.

In this book I offer a quick introduction to the real ways I have used the influence method to accomplish things in my career. Split into five chapters, each chapter explores ways to move past your position at work and acquire influence with your team that is real.

Building a relationship with your team will be possibly be uncomfortable as not everyone is ready or willing to bare their true self at work. Few companies have really grasped the power of engaging their teams as human beings first and as workers/employees second. I am fully aware that you might be working for a company right now that doesn't "get it". The only way around it is to do both. Tell your bosses want they want to hear, and build real relationships with your team too. The results you will achieve will speak for themselves.

So before we dive in, I want to thank you again for buying my book! I hope you enjoy it as much as I did writing it. I hope that you find it a resource in whatever career you find yourself in. Keep in mind that there will be people who may never "get it", and that's okay. We can't worry about those people. Build your tribe around the core values in this book and enjoy the results that will inevitably come with it!

CHAPTER 1:
COMMUNICATE

"I've learned that people will forget what you said, people will forget what you did, but people will never forget how you made them feel."

–*Maya Angelou*

Hearts and Minds

When it's your turn to speak, don't just pass on information, look to influence your audience. Shed the fear inside you, it is holding you back from being real, open and honest. Your tone and body language needs to be non threatening. There is a huge difference between manipulation and persuasion! Honey always gets more flies than vinegar.

When it's your turn to speak, don't just speak to pass on information but do so to build influence and credibility as a leader with your audience. Persuading an audience into believing you are worthy of their time and respect takes the gentle authority of speaking like a leader in the first place. Be mindful of your tone and body language. Your goal is to communicate credibility, not just to have the last word. Get the message across without trampling over other people in the process. A true leader does not have to speak or yell over other people to be heard, they are heard because people want to listen.

Fear based decision making is toxic because the goal of it is inherently negative. The fear we are talking about is one that originates in the mind of the leader who fears what may happen if they do not fall in line. It in its own way starts to manipulate and control them in return. When you are afraid for yourself and the consequences that may occur, you go into survival mode. It changes the way you look at people and situations – as things to be used and controlled. As puppets in your sick game, you are the only one that can win.

If we are to move on and modernize the world of work to become something other than a production line, we need to begin to address the huge problem of work sanctioned manipulation.

Some leaders do not have the ability or the mental fortitude to break this vicious cycle going on in their mind. For them, this is the only way to get something accomplished at work. They use their own fears and project it onto others by scaring them into action. When people are afraid, they shut down. They react by entering survival mode too. With everyone looking after their own skin, no one will see the benefit in forming any sort of long lasting bond with their team mates.

Fear is definitely a motivator, but not something you would ever want to use at work to influence other people. It becomes much harder to think of others and what they may be going through because you are only really concerned with your own welfare. Obviously, this cannot be the platform to use to influence your team to work hard for you.

The secret to persuading others is to offer them a choice. As you detail the fun and wild ride that is your mission, you need to ensure that participation is up to them. The choice to come along for the ride must be voluntary. It cannot be forced or demanded. Your audience needs to see the inherent value of what you are saying and get behind it.

Only when people see the reason to join with you will you get true particular situation, only you can know what to do. The thing to keep in mind is to understand that you need to really know your audience and to know what they want from you. This will take some soul searching and some honesty with yourself as you realize you may not have what it is they want right now. The only way to know is to initiate open dialogue and be honest with yourself and them.

If you are truly serious about perfecting the art of persuasion it will take some work on your part to figure out what your team needs and deliver it to them. If you do not yet have the skills or tools to do that, go out and get it. One of the best ways to persuade an audience that you do not yet understand is to ask them what they need and then deliver it. It will build trust and people will start to come around to the fact you just might the one who can be worth their time to follow.

Although it's easy for most people to just stick their head in the sand and ignore the world; we all want to be part of something more important than just day to day living. We are all looking for a place to belong, a place to relax and just ne ourselves with others that "get us".

You are the Brand

In the eyes, minds and hearts of the employees, you are the brand, you are the company. Employee loyalty and trust are based off of how you will treat them now and in the future. Integrity is choosing how to behave based on what you believe to be true and sticking by those values even when it's hard. Ethical leaders make choices with the group in mind and build followers organically.

Ever hear that old chestnut – people don't quit their job they quit their boss? It's true. The reason it's true has to do with how people relate to their company and workplace. For many people, how they feel about their job rests solely on how they feel about their boss. You and what you do or don't do come to reflect how your employees feel about their job as a whole.

The sobering reality is that people are not connected to the company in any real way. They are connected to the people in it. Their relationships and the quality of those relationships determine how they feel about the place they work at. If the relationship with their boss is sour or poisonous you can imagine how they feel about their work and themselves as an employee.

Customers do this too, of course. They base their feelings about a brand almost entirely on the interactions with the employees that serve them. If and when bad things happen, they can't help but associate all those negative feelings with the brand as a whole. With enough of these bad interactions and customers stop coming back altogether.

So think about what your personal 'brand' is. Your personal brand is how people feel when they interact with you. Consciously forming an idea of how you want to come across and be seen by others is paramount if you seek to influence them in any meaningful way. Think about how they will speak about you when you aren't around. Do they feel relieved or glad you aren't around? Or, do they miss you having you around and what you bring to the table?

It's time to dig deep and really think about how you come across to others. It takes a certain level of reflection and strength to come to terms with who you are as person, and how you want to come across to others as the leader.

Sometimes, people like you as a person, but despise you as their boss. That's a tough one to accept and look at. It can feel very painful that others see you as incompetent when in charge but think you are a nice person. On the other hand, the opposite could be true. They might really like you as their leader, but never want to hang out with you after work. They enjoy you as their boss and respect you – but will never see you as anything other than the boss. This world is getting so much more connected and social and to shun that trend risks losing your audience – your employees.

However, it's entirely possible to be both liked as a person and respected as their boss - it just takes a certain level of investment on your end to accomplish this. You'll need to build a relationship with your team that is based on some universal ethics, a personal code that will govern your actions.

Be kind, be respectful, and be honest with others. Let them in and be their support. Do the right thing simply because it is the right thing to do (something you will hear often in this book!).

Walking the Talk

Words are great but action is better. Communicate your positive intent by demonstrating it for others to see and witness. If you are full of hot air it will be obvious eventually. Demonstrate that you are here to win and will do what it takes to achieve that victory. No one expects you to be perfect, but they do expect you to pitch in and help.

Communicating your positive intent is best done by going out and doing it. Actions speak louder than words, so go out there and show them you mean it. It's not enough to simply have a plan and communicate that plan - you need to go out and make it come alive through action.

Standing shoulder to shoulder with your team in the trenches bypasses the lines of hierarchy and shows them you are serious about winning. It's a modern world, a transparent one. Hiding behind policy and hierarchy will hold you back more than it will help you. Do the right thing and help your employees on the floor, in the stockroom – where ever.

Sometimes we try to do the right thing and fail, and that's okay. If our intentions are good, it's much easier to get back on the horse and get keep going. Even though it seems everyone around you will expect superhuman perfection, trying to strive for it is pointless and impossible. Instead of killing yourself trying to keep up the appearance of invincibility, just do your best and do it with the right motivations. Eventually, your efforts will be noticed as you spend time with your employees and they get to see you as a person too, not just their boss. The real truth is they don't expect perfection, just dedication. They hope that you care and really do want to do the best job you can.

The stress of the business world and what it expects from its leaders can take a nasty toll on leaders who fail to equip themselves properly. Faced each day with the highly unrealistic task of delivering results and growth in key metrics regardless of the landscape or situation, some leaders simply go into survival mode. That kind of operational tunnel vision and selfish motivation does nothing to help their business succeed in the long run. The sad thing is some leaders do not know there is a better way. The better way is connect with others and share the burden of running the business. Open up and let them in, let them know what you need and ask for it.

We have all suffered at the hands of those leaders who take and take and take. Those kinds of leaders don't seem to understand the damage they are doing – or worse, don't care. And of course, they will find it hard to care when they keep themselves closed off from everyone. They can't see the damage they are doing in the long run for short term gains. The problem is they become addicted to the buzz, to the high of getting a win. Like a person abusing drugs, they are hurting themselves and others around them to get their next high, these leaders are in serious trouble.

The old ideas of command and control are still lingering poisons that companies and organizations can't seem to shed from their systems. Generally the boss does little work, and oversees the workers in their projects. Typically, the lower status people do the brunt of the work while the commanders, chiefs and bosses do very little actual work. When it comes time to pass out the medals and trophies, the bosses get all the praise with token lip service sometimes given to the team.

Practice what you preach to be true and go out and do it for real. Don't just talk about how you differ from others, demonstrate your positive intent by doing it and living it.. Stop hiding behind systems and hierarchy as reasons for inaction. If you are serious about impressing people that work for you, then you need to get your hands dirty and get to work.

The Human Factor

The quality of your interpersonal relationships is the deciding factor whether you will be successful or not. In order to be successful with people you need to bond with them and create a connection. Bonding builds affection and allows trust to flourish – which form the basic building blocks of successful teams. Time to look inward, and be vulnerable if you are serious about being the kind of leader this world needs.

It takes guts to bond with someone. You need to put yourself out there and risk being rejected. The risk is overcome with the reward of possibly connecting with someone. The rush of finding out someone else out there thinks like us, likes the same food or movies or maybe shares the same outlook on life is rewarding and the basis of human attachment.

The most common obstacle to bonding with other people is fear. Fear of what may happen or not happen. Just as in any other human relationship, we worry about what may happen or not happen if we do this or that. That kind of paralyzing fear can completely destroy any chance of reaching people in a meaningful way. The only way to conquer that fear is to admit it and to stop giving that fear a place to grow in your mind and heart. Face it, fight it and win.

Developing yourself is an important part of leadership, and letting go of your own issues that prevent you from reaching other people is paramount. Confront what it is you are afraid of and unpack it. Don't give your fear power by allowing it to fester like a wound. Open yourself up to those connections to reach out and be a person first and the boss second.

The quality of human relationships in our lives has a huge impact on our overall wellbeing. It helps develop our sense of self, our place in the world and affects how happy or content we are with life in general. It's not a stretch to say that we need other people, whether we want to admit it or not. There have been many studies done (not ones I will list here though, go google them!) that demonstrate in plain terms that we need other people to survive. Love, affection and human bonding are as important as water, food and shelter. The desire to belong and feel accepted by others runs deep in who we are as a species.

As we form bonds with other people trust and affection are the natural consequence. Bonding is the process of attachment. Mutual and interactive in nature, bonding is the glue that binds together individuals. Successful teams understand this and seek to build upon the natural bonding process that occurs when you spend enough time together as a group. Leaders have an important role in the bonding process.

Unfortunately, few leaders have ever created meaningful bonds themselves and so they would be hard pressed to see the value in creating those bonds. We can blame the corporate structures and systems that continuously reward antisocial behavior that are only concerned with results, and getting the best day in. When you are living day by day hour by hour you cannot stop and see the bigger picture.

Results speak for themselves right? Numbers on a page don't lie, right? Well they do, and they do often. They lie because they omit the truth of what it took to get those numbers in the first place. There is no balance sheet nor should there, be for team morale, team synergy or team skill. Those numbers didn't generate out of thin air; they were born from the hard work that the members of your team put in day in and day out.

Leaders are not rewarded for the bonds or comradery they have inspired in their teams rather they are rewarded based on how much money and transactions they pushed through that hour or day. If we are to see a change in this kind of behavior from our leaders, there needs to be a change in the way they are rewarded and also how they come to be seen as asset to the company.

CHAPTER 2: LISTEN

"Knowledge speaks, but wisdom listens"

–Jimi Hendrix

A Safe Harbor

Listening without judgment is hard to do. Sometimes we let that little voice in the back of our mind get a little too loud, drowning out the speaker altogether. A common thread that ties us all together is that we all want to be understood, to be heard, to be validated. Stop, drop and listen to actually hear what it is your employees are saying, not what you think they are saying.

Listening properly is one of the hardest skills to master when interacting with someone else. It takes practice because we often let our minds fill up with preconceived notions of what they speaker is trying to say. Jumping to conclusions usually has a negative impact on our ability to make the right choice. Instead of being proactive, it's a knee jerk or reactive decision, without much thought given to it.

Best thing to do is stay quiet both verbally, and mentally. Allow the person to finish, hear their words and guess their intention; and then set aside the time to process and digest what they are saying. Sometimes saying nothing is better than immediately responding with something just to fill up the silence. When you do eventually respond, repeat back what they said in your own words so that they know you were listening. Often saying that recap out loud with them also helps you get to see their side of things easier, if need be.

It's a reality of life that people are going to lie to you, probably more than you even think they do. However, to go around assuming everyone you meet is a liar and a cheat will do nothing for you. Keep in mind we have all been hurt before. No one's pain is bigger or more important than another's pain. So stop letting those past transgressions you have suffered from similar situations take hold of your life. Realize that things of your own creation could be the reason that prevents you from moving forward. You just might be your own worst enemy and biggest obstacle. If that were true, what would you do differently?

When employees come to you to talk about work or life, ensure that you are available for them. We have all heard the tired idea of an "open door policy". So have employees. No one really trusts the concept for the same reason you don't. Often leaders would use these 'open door' times to sort out who the problem employees are. In a moment the sad irony, the employee who takes a chance and decides to pour their heart out and voice their concerns or frustrations. The manager, with a gigantic and perfect smile, nods their head feigning interest. The manager isn't really listening at all – only really waiting for their turn to talk and shut them down with carefully crafted corporate responses. The employee may try and provide valid counterpoints, but to no avail – the manager isn't listening, and worse, has marked this employee as a trouble maker and "probably has to go" and be "promoted to customer."

Enough of these kinds of scenarios can really give a person some serious baggage. The stain left on your mind can be hard to wash away. You get the message loud and clear "I don't matter, my viewpoint is troublesome and I am not valid, got it". When their manager inevitably comes by and invites them in for a talk as part of their much vaunted "open door policy", the employee remembers to keep it light and offer no problems. The manager believes that there are no problems to fix, no dragons to slay. Unfortunately for literally everyone, there is so much wrong and by that point it may be too late.

Let's all agree that this practice needs a serious update and overhaul. Leaders, more often than not, fail to listen properly and instead allow their own issues cloud their minds, failing to truly hear the speaker. Instead of hearing what the employee is actually talking about, the leader is now convinced of ulterior motives and side plots. The employee is now viewed as a threat and must make the decision to either stop "complaining" or face serious consequences. Enough is enough, already.

Listen to your employees. Do so with a quiet mind, one free from fear and judgment. Understand that you are your own worst enemy and those things you think about another might be your own issues rearing their ugly head. Don't make decisions based on these emotions, because they are that, emotions. Emotions can and will cloud your viewpoint, especially if you already don't like someone. Be quiet and listen and hear the speaker. Repeat what they have said in your own words and be shocked that you might just come to another conclusion you weren't even expecting.

Remember that if there are indeed dragons to be slain, that it's easier with help. In order to get that help and fix a problem, you will need all the facts first and that will require time given to allowing the other person to speak fully and without interruption from you. The best part is you may be the only person that has ever listening to this speaker just, well speak. That in itself is invaluable. The loyalty and bond they will show you afterwards are hard to come by. This is influence building at its best.

Trust Issues

Trust is a valuable yet fragile thing. Handle it wrong and it can all fall to pieces right in your hand. Trust is hard to win and easily lost. Work hard to be worthy of trust and protect it once you acquire it. Trust creates the possibility of deeper relationships than simply talking about the weather and what they ate for supper last night. Once the walls are down, the real work can begin as you forge long lasting partnerships with your team.

The vast majority of employees out there, right now, do not trust their boss. They don't trust their company. Bosses have generally shown themselves to be untrustworthy with how they have treated their employees over the years. Sadly many bosses out there have abused the trust of their employees for personal gain and that leaves a deep scar in the minds of the affected employees. When employees feel that their boss is out to get them, they will shut down to protect what dignity is left and will never offer their best again.

Building trust is hard to do. Our natural tendency is to stay behind our protective barriers as we interact with people. Think of it as a kind of human firewall that prevents possible threats to infect us with their nonsense. Employees of course will naturally view you with suspicion at first. It's your job to ensure that you come across as someone who is not a threat to their safety and someone worth letting down their guard for.

Imagine you are starting a new job, and meeting the team for the first time. Chances are most of the employees you meet will be reserved and cautiously optimistic as they silently study you for clues as to what kind of boss you are going to be. They are usually hoping that you are a nice person, not too hardcore with the rules and will work hard. Truth is they can't help but worry that you might just be like all the other bosses they have ever had – egotistical jerks who care only about their bonus, exclusive parking space and to make their lives miserable as you sit in your office doing nothing all day.

Employees are depending on you to be different from all the rest even if they can't articulate it. It's your job and calling to be different, to be the kind of leader they want and need. So what can you do to change their minds and hearts? What are the ways to build trust with your employees so that they come to know you as someone who cares about them? It's the small things.

Just like any other human relationship, work relationships need the same care and attention if they are to thrive. Trust being the foundation of any good relationship, it would make sense to ensure that your employees and peers know that you are trustworthy. So, how to go about making sure of this? Well, the simplest answer is to demonstrate it with actions. Simply telling them that you are will not do the trick. They need to see it and feel it to believe it.

A major reason why employees do not trust their boss is that they have felt abandoned by them more than once. Bosses who have a skewed sense of entitlement to not pull their weight will really leave employees resentful of the whole chain of command. Feeling abandoned by another really messes with your self-esteem and you definitely cannot help resenting the person who abandoned you. Those feelings of being left to die don't do anything to build trust, but rather destroy it.

So, what does this have to with listening? Listening is not just one on one in a room at a predesignated time period; it's the ongoing series of smaller conversations that happen throughout the day. The major reason that employees feel alienated and alone is due to the fact that the lines of communication are severed between them and their boss. The line is severed when bosses do not stop to listen and find out what it is their team needs from them. Leaders who do not build trust by listening to the needs of their team will never make them feel safe. That's the key, really. The point of using your ability to find out what they need is to build trust and offer them the safety they have been looking for. It's nearly impossible to offer help and support and deliver on what someone needs from you and leave them still feeling left out in the cold.

Leaders that offer genuine safety, build trust with their employees. We aren't talking job security, here. Safety is the sense that you are providing what the employees need from you as someone in charge. It can be as simple as providing backup support on the POS on a busy Saturday, or ensuring they get their time off so they can take that summer trip to Cuba.

So if you take anything away from this, remember that in order to build trust with your team you need to stop and listen to them and find out what it is they need from you. If you make this part of how you run your ship you will develop their trust in you and make them feel safe with you as their captain. Remember it's the small things that count. Do your best to deliver what they need from you and always be open to chat and listen. Be available! Don't just say that you are available – do it for real and make time for them. This is how you can also build a sense of who you are as a leader. Your employees will talk amongst themselves and talk about you in a favorable light.

We're in this Together

Problems facing your company or store are easy to fix if you know where to start. Leverage the experience and insights of those people working on the frontlines. They are the ones who know exactly what is working and what is not. More often than not they already have a solution or know how to find it. A strong leader who isn't afraid to ask for help will confidently face and overcome obstacles.

Crowd sourcing your solutions to common problems facing the team is a great way to get your team involved in fixing what could be wrong. Fix problems and prevent future ones by utilizing the experience and knowledge of your team mates that do the real work each and every day. The front line employees have seen it all and most likely have the best solutions to common issues or bottlenecks bogging down the company.

Keep the lines open and ask how things are going often and take their feedback seriously. You may not be able to fix or change everything they find annoying, but do your best. Also, if you cannot fix something or change policy, let them know and why you can't. That kind of honesty is hard to come by in the corporate world and your team will appreciate your frank and open communication as it's so very rare.

Companies love to talk about how innovative and transparent they are but rarely do they actually act on the feedback they receive. Why? It takes a lot of guts to admit something isn't working; some companies just can't come to grips with the fact that they have spent a great deal of money figuring out a solution to a problem only to then learn it isn't working out after all.

Fixing problems in real time takes a careful mix of experience and intuition to come up with the right course of action. Solving issues before they become real problems allows you to stay proactive and one step ahead. Proactive leaders also are much calmer; more relaxed and have a developed confidence in themselves. Far too many leaders fall prey to their emotions and allow these emotions to cloud their vision and make poor decisions as a result.

Make it a point to include your employees into your decision making process. Ask them what they think and pick their brains as to what they would do to fix the issues. Keep the lines of communication open and fluid. Do your best to let them speak their mind and to create a culture of cooperation and communal success.

It should be no secret by now that your best competitive advantage lies with the people that work for you. They alone have the skills to help you succeed and overcome problems if you would only stop and listen properly. Fall back on the experience and viewpoint of your frontline team mates. Chances are they already have the solution and just need someone to come along and make it happen.

Leave your ego at the door. Do not get in the way of your own progress by shutting down the experiences of those who have done or are doing it every day. Leaders who feel threatened in their position will fail to listen properly and continually to the people that work for them and with them.

Feeling Validated

It's a common mistake to believe that listening is only done with a pair of ears. Few people master the ability to listen fully. True listening involves all the ways we can connect with another person. Listen with your heart, mind and ears if you really are interested in hearing someone completely. Start by listening to yourself and understanding where you stand if you hope to help others do the same and validate other people in your life.

Few people listen with more than their ears. As a basic human need and desire, we all want to feel validated and to be accepted. Those feelings of validation drive our behavior as we seek out experiences and live our life. To be truly accepted by another person is a wonderful thing and sparks human connection known as bonding.

As the leader, remember that you are ultimately leading other human beings who all want the same things out of life. Even if at times it may feel like you need to turn off your human side to make 'the right choice' never completely turn it all off. If you do, you will forget what it means to be alive. You are not a robot, you have feelings and emotions. Your employees are not robots either, and will need to be treated as people as you make decisions concerning their work day.

Never miss an opportunity to really connect with your team as people and validate their existence through meaningful and real conversation. Embrace them as people and connect as people first; coworkers second. Listen to them. Make time and space for you to talk with them one on one. Push distractions away and really open up to the idea and possibility of creating a bridge to the other person and allow them to feel that they can do the same with you.

Listening to your employees and accepting them for who they are can only help you to become a better leader. Employees are usually patronized and mostly ignored by most leaders they have worked for in the past. They have come to expect that they will never be really heard or acknowledged as a person. Do the opposite. Embrace your employees and engage them in discussion. Listen to what they say and be a human being.

Great communication takes great listening skills. For both you and your team making listening to each other as people first can only help to build synergy and comradery. These two things will strengthen the ability to work as a team in a cohesive way that is not forced or phony. People that enjoy working together work harder for one another. That unspoken bond between team mates that simply know what the other is thinking are powerful teams that like to win. Who wouldn't want a team like that?

Employees go through a lot during the week and do not need or want your sympathy. They do want your support and to know that you advocate for them on their behalf. Be respectful of their requests for days off, vacation time and whatever else they might need from you. Always look for ways to challenge your team and continue to improve them, but never at the cost of their happiness. A happy employee will always work harder, do more and ask for less than one that is not happy with their lot at work. If a certain position bores them or upsets them, see if you can work with them to move them to different area, position or department.

Never reject or ignore someone's thoughts, feelings or emotions. Listen to what they are saying and work with them to find a solution. Sometimes the easiest fix is to be the listener and hear them out. Often once people hear themselves talk out their problem aloud they come to their own solutions. Be available and ready to be the shoulder your team needs. They will thank you for it.

CHAPTER 3: ENGAGE

"Always treat your employees exactly as you want them to treat your best customers."

-Stephen R. Covey

Generation ME

Leaders who fail to engage their millennial employees are shooting themselves in the foot. Many companies fail to understand the huge potential millennials and the generations after them have to offer. What do they want? Meaning! They are much more enlightened than you might give them credit for. They are hungry to find work that speaks to them and their skillsets. Ironically, companies say they want people who will buy into their mission statement, yet fail to understand that the millennials want exactly that – something to believe in. Give it to them and reap the rewards.

Millennials are a group of young people that have built quite the negative reputation for themselves in the world of work. They continue to confuse, confound and generally infuriate leaders and companies who employ them. That is of course, until you try and understand their situation and choose to engage them in the way they need to be, and maybe not the way they want to be. Chances are if you are a leader you have had to manage these folks, or maybe you are one of them!

So, what do the millennials want, anyways? What will make them happy and motivated in order for them to give their best each and every day at work? Just like their relationship status on Facebook, it's complicated.

In order to understand them, you need to get where they are coming from. Even if you do not understand them, at least make the effort to really dig deep into why they have the world view they do. In order to keep it brief and stay on point with how to influence them, we need to understand two major aspects of their upbringing that has forged the way they carry themselves at work and in life.

The first issue is the general failure of proper parenting. The truth is that parenting went through a period of insanity, and still ongoing. These kids have grown up being told their whole life that they are a special unique snowflake that can do anything they want to do in life. All they have to do is go out and get it if they want it. This total disregard for preexisting systems and a total lack of accountability has allowed the millennial generation to grow up to feel entitled and special far beyond what is reasonable. No wonder they think can get whatever it is they want no matter how far-fetched – their whole life has been a lie directed towards that falsehood. The truth you can't just go out and get what you want simply because you want it. It has never worked that way and never will.

Imagine the anger and despair a millennial feels when they come crashing into the walls of reality as they start to understand they have been lied to all their life? You might start to understand why as an adult they are moody, sullen and reserved in their approach to well, everything. This is where they get their deep mistrust of official institutions and dogmatic thinking. They are starting to figure things out and are not happy that they have been fed lies and half truths about the way the world operates. So take care and allow yourself to be empathetic to the existential struggle they are still wrangling with as they go to work for you each day.

The second major theme to understand about millennials is their general impatience about life in general. Much of us remember a time with no internet, no texting, no Facebook. Most of these kids do not have such memories. They have grown up in and have been raised in a world of instant gratification. The dopamine highs of being validated in the blink of an eye are something some of us can't even understand let alone appreciate. Life doesn't happen at the speed of Twitter, life is bit more substantial than what can be said in 140 characters. Life is messy, it's ugly and it's slow paced. You can't put a filter on life and hide behind it.

To make things worse, it's for some the only way to feel beautiful, powerful, and validated as a person. Social media and phones have made connecting with other people in a meaningful way harder than ever before. We have kids growing up into adults who don't even know how to form real relationships. Their hookup culture they have grown accustomed to, does not lend itself very well in forming meaningful bonds. Sadly many teenagers don't or can't even rely on their friends when they go through tough times. Their friends too are going through their own things too and lack coping mechanisms of their own. This is the blind truly leading the blind.

Enter the world of work. Things happen slowly, you find out that you can't be the CEO in 6 months. It can be hard to make an impact as a cashier at a grocery store or find the deeper meaning of life in selling a pair of socks to a rude granny. Working a job that pays minimum wage is not exactly glamourous. Cleaning toilets and scrubbing floors is not something cool to share on your Facebook timeline. Going to university and realizing you cannot land that dream job you always wanted and end up working at Starbucks where you are screamed at by that crazy lady who wants perfect foam on her latte can crush your soul – if you let it.

Work to understand where your millennial employees are coming from and learn how to engage them in ways they can appreciate. They are coming at things from an angle most likely different than you. It's entirely possible they can't appreciate the way you see the world, at least not yet.

Millennials are absolutely worth the effort - so engage them on terms they will understand, as they could very well become your best employees. They are after all seeking meaning and direction in a world seemingly drowning in fakeness. They want something to believe in, a cause to take up and make their own, just like any of us. Millennials want to be part of something bigger than themselves and once they have been properly engaged will work tirelessly to see those values come to life in their work.

Embrace them, engage them, and ultimately involve them. Take the time to explain your point of view and give them the stage to explain theirs.

They will love the fact you have shown them respect and they will show it back in kind.

Millennials and the generations after them will continue to seek employment that falls within these guidelines and beyond. Gone are the old ways of work of masters and slaves. Folks, it's time to embrace the future and adapt accordingly or fall behind and become obsolete. The world of work is changing for the better, embrace it and leverage the influence you build with your team and further your leadership goals.

The Likeable Leader

Leaders who engage others with the right mindset will build teams based on a hardy combination of mutual respect and admiration. Soft power is superior to hard power when it comes to other human beings. Soft power attracts followers with the offer of mutual benefit through cooperation. Influence people using persuasion, and get your team to work hard for you, because they want to, not because they have to.

When it comes to influencing someone, it's better to be liked that hated. Likable people are easier to get along with and much easier to say yes to. Consciously make the effort to just relax and embrace your social side, and build influence naturally with other people. People naturally follow someone they like and admire, not someone they are afraid of.

Contrary to popular belief, leadership is definitely a popularity contest at times. Just not the way you might think. You aren't trying to be everyone's friend, but you need to be friendly and approachable. Employees who like their boss come to respect them, and admire them and will work harder to impress and support their boss because of their relationship with them. Create and defend a work environment that is both fun and productive. Be the kind of boss that your employees will brag about and feel good about working for.

Soft power is superior and should always be used instead of hard power, which relies on threats and force to accomplish goals. Fear is a corrosive motivator, and the stress it causing eats away at the confidence and wellbeing of those that suffer under it. Forcing other people to do what you want is not the way to lead. Sometimes people need to be gently reminded you are in charge, but that shouldn't be the norm. If you have to constantly remind people you are the one in charge, you probably don't have any leadership influence over them at all.

Persuasion based leadership is about offering your potential and current followers a choice. The choice to follow you has to be their choice; you cannot force them to fall in line. The employee may comply with what you want, but their attitude inside will not change and in fact may even sour towards you. Forcing someone to comply will over time build up their resentment towards you. That resentment bubbles up to the surface and takes shape in different ways, almost always negative. Lower productivity, job apathy, etc. An otherwise stellar employee fights back by disengaging from you and their work.

We have all had bosses that made us feel terrible about ourselves, that drive us so completely crazy we literally hated them. They made us feel that we couldn't do our job and nothing was ever good enough. Each day after dealing with a boss like that we went home drained, angry and frustrated. We dreaded having to go back in the next day and go through all that hell all over again. Do you really want to continue this nonsense? Do you really want to be yet again that kind of boss you is a bully instead of the teacher? Break the vicious cycle; be the difference that people see and feel when they work for you.

Embracing likeability is your best way to get over the archaic leadership ideals of the past and build a relationship with your team that allows you to have them come along willingly.

A Spark in their Heart

Motivating others is less mystifying when you understand that you cannot apply a 'one size fits' all policy regarding it. What might motivate one person, does not necessarily motivate another. Money can be a motivator, but does not have the staying power of other methods. Find out what motivates your individual team mates through real and meaningful engagement will allow you unlock their potential.

Motivation is perplexing if you try to understand what someone wants without the context of who you are trying to influence. What may motivate someone to succeed, doesn't always do the same for another. It all boils down to consequences. The reason someone may work harder than another or care more than another is about a personal endgame that individual has cultivated in their mind. Usually, it's bigger than the work itself. Most often what drives people forward is the underlying meaning, the bigger picture of it all.

Money is a motivator most of the time, and for good reason. Money creates access to things we need to live. It can also uphold a certain lifestyle that we want. Again, it comes down to personal context. For most people money is an issue until it isn't. Money will eventually have a diminishing return. More often than not the richest people are the least fulfilled, as they can buy people, things and experiences but they cannot buy meaning – that's something they have to find on their own.

The truth is sometimes the pain of not moving forward with a new strategy outweighs the pleasure of sitting in the mud. Few people enjoy going to the gym, but some do. Those that do have gotten the results they have been looking for or at least are seeing some sort of improvement that drives them on. One day you wake up and look in the mirror and are no longer cool with the person staring back at you. You decide to make a life decision because you value life and health. Or maybe, you value the fact that being in shape will make you more attractive. Whatever the reason for making the switch in what you are currently doing, it's a personal one. You alone have to make the connection between what is and what is not working.

At work people come to work for you and the company for many different reasons. It's ultimately up to you to find out what those reasons are. Once you find out what those reasons are for each member of the team you can better craft individual approaches to spark motivation in their heart. Trying a blanket approach and making policy with generalizations don't really work for reasons we already discussed. Take the time to build a relationship with your team and find out what makes them tick and what drives them forward.

Leadership experts have pondered this mysterious force known as motivation for decades. The fact is motivation is personal and will naturally be different for everyone you encounter out there. This is why building a relationship with your team is not pirely a social one, but an effective way to peel back the layers of the people you work with to see all the working gears and pulleys of their mind and heart. Then and only then can you hope to see what drives them.

Mutually Beneficial

When it comes to basic human bonding, reciprocity is possibly the best way to go about it. Doing something nice for someone has the effect of having that gesture reciprocated in kind. The very concept of the company is an example of a mutually beneficial arrangement. Companies need employees to generate revenue, employees use companies to generate income. Both parties need each other. Forget the tired concept of master and slave and embrace the new symbiotic way of thinking about your employees.

Reciprocity is the social obligation to give or offer back the same treatment in kind that was received. If someone does a nice thing for us, we feel inclined to do it back. Generally, when someone does something nice for us, we think well of them. Humans are most certainly hardwired to see acts of generosity as innately good. The natural tendency of a healthy mind is to find a way to repay that kind gesture with a kind gesture of your own.

The opposite is also true. Employees who have had bad experiences with you or other bosses are less likely to trust you and be less likely to share their best self with you. The act of reciprocating is demonstrating that you are trustworthy. Instead of just saying that you are worth their time and trust, you go about to prove it with kind acts and gestures. Imagine the pointless waste of time trying to get someone to believe in you when you haven't done anything to prove you are worthy of it.

This is why it's important to treat others around you as well as possible not only because it might come back to haunt you one day; but also because it's the right thing to do. It's a sobering and sad fact that doing the right thing and following ethics and morality can put you at odds with your company. Often the business model that guides the decision making of your company does not have the best interest in mind for the group, but a select few instead. In a publicly traded company, one on the stock market, it can be nearly impossible to stay true to ethical leadership. In this kind of familiar setting, the power is not with the average worker doing the real work, but rests with the shareholder. They alone pull the strings and guide the company along its path to profits. Infinite business growth is the unicorn of our financial forests.

Leaders often grapple with their own morality as they make decisions to follow the company line or forge their own way. When a company is morally bankrupt employees will not offer their best self as they will be too busy defending themselves. This is true anywhere. If a friend has let you down time and time again, are you willing to imagine that the next time will be any different? You may want to believe that it will, but their track record says otherwise.

Symbiotic relationships benefit both parties involved. Each member in the relationship gets access to something they need from the other. A kind of balance and acceptance of each other develops as both parties realize they need each other and are better off cooperating than being apart. An obvious example of this kind of symbiosis is the company and the employee, and to a lesser extent the customer, too. The purpose of the company is to sell goods or services to customers for a profit. If the company stops turning a profit long enough, it goes bankrupt, and essentially dies. Typically, people choose to become an employee when they want to generate income. Normally, the employee trades their time for money. This is a basic form of symbiotic relationship that exists in the working world, yet so few companies really understand that relationship well enough.

In reality, companies operate on more of a master and slave relationship than a symbiotic one. Lip service is often given to their employees when a record breaking quarter for profits is announced. You can be sure that if sales do slump or targets aren't met, it's always the fault of the employees. Sound familiar?

No matter what you are selling, people will always be your competitive edge. Believe it and know it. Just as we are asking you to form a relationship with your employees in order to influence them and get them to rally to your banner, the same is true for customers. Customers interact with your company and brand as a whole through the employees they interact with. The fact is, you need great employees. You need employees who are skilled, able and willing to carry out all and more of what you need them to each and every day.

The only way you can expect to get them to do this is to engage them in the most basic form of give and take. Treat your employees well, take care of them and pay them appropriately. Do not look at them as some sort of liability, but rather, the edge you can use fall back on to defeat your rivals.

CHAPTER 4: AWARENESS

"The ultimate value of life depends upon awareness and the power of contemplation rather than upon mere survival"

- Aristotle

Looking Inside Out

Self-awareness is the dual realization that you are both separate and connected from everyone else. Having a high self-awareness gives you the powerful edge when it comes to understanding other people and what makes them tick. People after all are complicated, and their reasons for doing this or that are many. Look deep inside your mind and push out doubt and fear, which are obstacles to connection with others. Stay cool, calm and collected when the bullets start flying – your team will need you to lead the way with a steady hand.

In order to know others well you need to know yourself well. Understanding your own talents, strengths, motivations and what drives you forward will allow you to understand the same in others around you. If you hope to influence others you need to know what makes them tick and what drives them. The first place to start is with yourself, and to look inside and ask some tough questions about what makes you do what you do. It's also important to know what scares you and how that can act as a motivator, or obstacle.

A common conundrum is that you are swayed and influenced by your own inner dialogue. That inner voice has a lot to say and can directly impact how you interact with the world. You have a personal bias that acts as a filter allowing certain viewpoints in and certain ones out. What you come to hold as true or valuable in life is influenced by these filters. Some people do not even realize they have these filters and take for granted the fact they see things a certain way and others do not. The dangerous line of thinking is to take belief systems or opinions as fact and make life choices around them. Facts are facts whether you want to acknowledge it or not.

Start by evaluating what you believe to be true and false about the world and the people that live in it. If you are honest with yourself about all of it, you might just come to some conclusions you are not ready for. And that's completely fine, if not ideal. It's ideal because it means you have allowed yourself to be open and willing to accept new information and a new perspective without feeling threatened. Priming the soil in your mind for new things to grow is a great first step to observing the world with new eyes.

Chances are what drives you forward may not drive another person in the same way. Like we have mentioned before, motivation is a personal thing and the reasons for doing this or that are many. Reading others is a skill that is developed with practice. It's something that might even take a life to master but it offers you a keyhole to look through and gaze upon a new world you might haven't thought of before – the realization that others around you are all leading rich and complex lives completely separate of your own. Sure, we all know people are doing their own thing and are facing hardships, but the realization of that and the deeper knowledge of that is what you want to achieve.

Contemplation of how other people are all connected in a vast web will definitely clear out any notions of you being alone in the world. When you embrace this idea, you can read people well and know why they do what they do, even if they may not know it yet for themselves. This is how you can act as a teacher to those who do not know that they have much to learn still. Lastly, looking inside yourself to understand the world creates a space in your mind that, when built upon over time, can be your sanctuary from the storm.

A calm leader makes better decisions. They draw upon a solid foundation and are not easily swayed by their emotions no matter what goes on around them. Imagine a scenario at work or somewhere else in your life that could upset you and cause you to get emotional. It could be anything minor, all the way up to a major life event. Reflect on what you might do or say. Do you know how you will react? Chances are you would like to think you might be calm and cool under fire. Often times we are not because we have not allowed space in our mind to play out these types of scenarios or think about how we would react. Most of us just simply react and muddle through it. Try this little exercise to build your own calm place in your mind as a kind of 'thought dojo'. In this mental dojo you can spar with and better prepare for what may happen, just like a warrior would.

Remember that your team will look to you in a crisis; you cannot lose your cool and fall prey to emotion. Stay stoic and calm, be proactive and thoughtful. Mental toughness is in short supply today. People are too easily swayed by their emotions and allow themselves to get riled up over small things. Face down your fear and doubt in the dojo of the mind. Do not let others see the storm of doubt that rages inside you. Be the one who knows the way through. Remind your team it will be okay and see that it will be. Leverage the wisdom that comes from contemplation of your own struggle to better help others with their own battle.

Going with Your Gut

Intuition is the art and skill of 'knowing what will happen before it happens. Considering all the actors and factors that can influence the outcome, you better judge how things will actually play out in the real world. Intuitive leadership is the result of experience blended, actual ability with a touch of skill. Intuitive thinking is usually dismissed as it means choosing a path without sufficient proof or hard evidence. It takes guts to go with your gut. Remember that the world was not moved by people who stood still.

Intuition is the art of knowing what may happen before it does. Even if what you imagined to happen doesn't, you have better prepared for the future. Intuitive thinking is based upon experience and probability. These are two important factors for success in the business world let alone your own life.

Experience can help fortify you against doubt and worry as you know how things might play out as you have done it or seen it before. Probability is based on knowing how things are interconnected and how they can affect each other in some way.

Leaders who rely on the complex mix of experience and their own knowledge of how the world works are intuitive leaders. Interestingly, few companies grasp or tolerate leaders who act like leaders. Leadership is about change and flux, management is about compliance and following the rules. Knowing that something is not working is not always convenient for those who have put into place that policy or ideology. It's hard to feel sympathy for those that would rather rot in the safety of their cave than face the bright sun outside.

The leader who listens to themselves and forges their path based on their intuitive inner voice is one with the courage to properly lead. Courage is doing something that may be scary and doing it anyway. You can't always be safe and numb to the dangers around you. It takes a certain kind of someone to shoulder that burden and be the one to break new ground. It's time we stop asking leaders to be leaders and then slap them on the wrist or worse when they act like leaders. Do you want compliance? Or, do you seek to transform the status quo? One of these has to give to allow the other to happen.

Intuition gives our species a sort of time machine for the mind, a window into the future. You can imagine our ancestors talking amongst themselves as they notice some movement in the tall grasses. Is it a lion or wild boar? They had three options, fight, flee or explore the grass and find out. Ultimately, the people who got it right are the ones that we call our ancestors. So there is something to be said for those who made the right choice without all the right evidence.

Sometimes you cannot be certain how to proceed, but the world won't wait for you. Events happen in real time and cannot be paused. How you choose to react is based on how much you have allowed yourself to consider all the factors at play. Cultivating your own intuition takes time, experience and a little trial and error. Do not be dismayed if things do not always go your way, that's life. Standing in one place won't get you very far either.

Empathy is not Sympathy

Empathy is feeling with someone, sympathy is feeling for someone. Sympathy does nothing to bond with the other person, who is in pain or distress, rather a cold and callous "sucks to be you". Despite the commonly held idea that being empathy equates weakness, it couldn't be further from the truth. In fact, all the qualities and characteristics that a successful and modern business will need rest upon a strong moral foundation with empathy as its core.

Empathy and sympathy are two very different things. They are often confused for being interchangeable and nothing could be farther from the truth.

Empathy is feeling with someone. Empathy is the knowledge and capacity to understand what the other person is going through. Seeing the world from another's perspective is powerful, but knowing also what the other person is feeling and feeling it with them is the epitome of bonding. Feeling safe enough to trust someone with your pain takes a leap of faith and trust. Sharing that pain and having it not understood or empathically reciprocated can be devastating to the person who shared.

All of us are rolling around out there in a stormy sea called "life". We all want a safe place to dock our ships at and be sheltered from the rain, wind and darkness. We all come to the table a little broken, a little bruised. Empathy is the shared awareness that we all are flawed humans, who make mistakes and are all fighting to stay afloat in that stormy ocean. It's comforting to know you aren't alone out there; you aren't the only person struggling. When you extend your hand and offer help, support and the awareness of "I've gone through that too" you create a bridge to the other person.

Sympathy on the other hand is quite different than empathy. Sympathy is feeling for someone, but not making the attempt to really be there for the person who is hurting. It's a kind of emotional drive by shooting. It hurts because it's phony, an impersonal and cold way of faking connection. The mistake is trying to offer condolence where it is not wanted or valued.

There are some things that will happen that no matter what you say, it will never be fixed or get better. When someone is going through something very personal and you know about it, the worst thing you can do is offer trite sympathy. In this case, know that sometimes you can't do anything but simply be there. It's not what you say or don't say that matters; it's that you are there for the person and allowing them the safety to share their pain with you that matters most.

Empathy is a choice, a choice to bond with the other person. Sympathy is also a choice, but it's one of inaction. So as a leader you can choose to bond and offer safety, or create further isolation through callous sympathy. It stands to reason that if you take a chance to connect with someone else and share your pain and it goes poorly, you'll be much more cautious in the future. This is what sympathy does. It fakes the feelings of what empathy really does in place of never going out on a limb yourself as the listener. Imagine a world of people never engaging one another empathically? Unfortunately, that world is the world we live in today. With so many people consumed with their own narcissism, it's nearly impossible to give a damn about someone else. That's the sad fact of our modern world. This obsession with ME find its way into the world of work as leaders who don't value connection and bonding think only of themselves and are too afraid to bond and put themselves out there in an empathic way. This is why teams across the globe are disconnecting and disengaging from their jobs. They are protecting themselves as they see no safe harbor at work to dock their ship at.

Realize the immense strength of character in showing your hand instead of offering your fist. Step outside of your own problems and create a safe space on your shoulder for others to rest upon. Allow others to fall to pieces with you and help them build themselves back up again.

Sometimes you are a sounding board so they can talk out what is bothering them, and other times you need to help them figure things out with them.

You can't just be their boss; you need to be a person too.

Time to Get Real

The brutal truth that people are expected to so much more with so much less is taxing and takes its toll on body and spirit. Long hours, low pay and tedious monotony can make the service industry feel more like the slavery industry. In order to get people to truly care, build your leadership framework on shared contribution and a strong moral ethic that will always supersede a mission statement on the wall. People don't truly follow an ideal, they follow a person. Be someone worth following.

Many companies out there still operate like its 1965. Long hours, minimum wage and tedious drudgery are what the modern worker still has to deal with on a daily basis. Factor in the fact that customers are more impatient, more likely to lose their cool, and generally more unrealistic as time goes on. The work is emotionally draining, physically demanding and pays terrible.

Is it any wonder why employee engagement is so bad? Then on top of all of this, we have terrible leaders making the lives of their employees even more miserable. These leaders are generally uncaring, mean and demanding. Pushing and pulling their employees until they quit. And those same managers scratch their collective heads as they stare at their 70% turnover rates.

A massive part of employee engagement is based on how they feel they are treated by their managers. As the saying goes, "people don't quit their job, they quit their boss." Most managers don't give a second thought to treating their employees like playing pieces on their chessboard. If a pawn dies, that's okay. That's what they are there for, right? To be used and abused until they eventually die? After all they are just a playing piece for the player, a means to an end. Dramatic comparisons aside, this kind of mentality is rampant throughout all workplaces retail and the trades being possibly the best/worst example of it.

In order to get your people to care and like their job they need to like you and the place they work at. Seems easy enough except so many companies don't seem to get it, do they? This is because so many of these same companies don't build a foundation for sustainable business to be built upon. If you treat your people as disposable objects eventually they will just act that way and give you nothing in return. After all, why should they? What's in it for them?

That's what you must answer every day you work with your team on the floor – what's in it for them? If you can successfully answer that without talking about monetary compensation you are well on your way to getting your head around employee engagement. Generally people don't care about money as much as they care about meaningful work. The work doesn't have to move mountains and change the world it just has to be connected to something that is bigger than them.

The hard and brutal truth is that sometimes work sucks, no matter what you do or don't do. Sometimes it's nothing you have done or not done. Remember that people work for you, and they aren't invincible. Things will get to them, they will get tired and sick. People don't work for their companies; they work for their bosses and coworkers at those companies. Keep yourself grounded when you engage your team each day. Don't let the stress get to you either. Part of being the boss means overcoming what gets you down so that you have the strength to help others up when they eventually fall.

CHAPTER 5: RESPECT

"Knowledge will give you power, but character – respect." *-Bruce Lee*

The Two Way Street

Respect is a two way street, as it should be. In order to gain respect you need to show it and be worthy of it. Be a good person for the sake of it, not for what it will get you. Respect is not a trophy to place on your mantle; it's the natural consequence of ethical leadership.

Respect is a feeling of admiration towards another person that share a common value system. If you value that person and who they are, you will come to respect them as a natural consequence. The misconception that respect is based on titles or hierarchy is a dangerous one because it can warp the way a leader behaves when in a position of power. The real measure of your capacity to be respected will be based on how you treat other people. This is especially true when those same people have nothing to offer you in return or cannot help you get something or somewhere.

Consistency of character is perhaps the most important piece of the puzzle in keeping yourself held in high regard. You cannot simply blow up at someone and then quickly apologize and expect no damage to be done to that relationship. While it's sometimes hard to stay consistent you need to always work towards it. We are all human and we all make mistakes and slip up from time to time.

Never be above being the first one to apologize. We all make mistakes and you will be no different. You will however be judged on how you handle yourself after the mistake has been made. So take care to realize this and embrace your own fallibility by owning up to your mistake. Own it, and also make up for it. Make it right and do things to avoid it happening where possible. How you choose to handle conflict will signal what kind of person you are and what kind of boss you will be. You can't always be right, so abandon that pointlessly proud viewpoint. The person who has never made a mistake has never tried, after all.

Respect is not something to be acquired. It ebbs and flows, naturally. You can gain it and lose it quickly, so don't fall into the trap of thinking you can sit on your laurels once you have felt that you have acquired someone's respect. Their opinions and values will change and possibly might deviate from yours. You can fall off being on the same page with people and find yourself at odds with someone who no longer shares the same value system that brought you together. So don't go chasing the respect of others, but instead be a good person and do your best to do well by other people and your influence will continue to grow and stay resilient despite a change in the weather.

No matter where you find yourself out there in the working world, people need to be shown respect and to feel valued. Taking action to value others with respect shows your employees you are there to play ball, not just to play house. It sends a message that you are not like all the other deadbeat managers who have hurt them and used them in the past. You are standing tall and declaring "I see you, I value you, and I want you to succeed". Nothing is more demeaning that being treated as if you are expendable, useless and invisible.

A Values Based Proposition

Our values shape how we view the world. We perceive the world and what is important to us through the filter of our values. Naturally, we tend to gravitate towards others that share similar values and viewpoints. These are the people we form close bonds with as they understand and share what is important and as we see it, inherently valuable. It is this shared experience that allows mutual respect to flourish and grow. .

When we talk about team building, we are really talking about tribe building. Leaders build their tribe around shared value systems, a common viewpoint of how the world operates. Don't focus on the differences of why people may not fit together, but rather what they share in common.

Leaders who do not understand this can get bogged down by these differences and forget what is important. Unity will not happen overnight, it takes time so invest it well.

Fundamental differences in worldviews are recipes for conflict and discord not only at work but also in life. Within any group, conflict is inevitable. A breakdown in communication is the source of most conflict. As the leader of the group it's your role and responsibility to remove barriers to communication and to remedy the conflicts that arise regardless. Many times the source of the conflict is a trivial matter where the two parties did not see eye to eye. When mediating such things it's important to point out both why the conflict arose, and to reinforce the crucial fact that *"we're all playing on the same team and all want to win."* Sometimes how we want to go about it may differ, but the knowledge that we are all in this for the same outcome will unify the team when the details divide them.

Personality clashes will always be a bone of contention, some people just don't play nice together and there is little you can do about it.

Even when both parties understand each other, there can still be bad blood that prevents them from just getting on with the day. The need to be right, the need to get the last word, the need to one up the other can make full grown adults act like squabbling children. Expect that these situations will flare up and be ready to deal with it when it does, because they will. While they can be distracting and a great source of nonsense, mediating it and just simply dealing with it head on sometimes has the benefit of finally resolving whatever the issues were to begin with. Even if the matters weren't resolved, often once the parties have been heard and allowed to voice their issues, the matter might die down.

Team cohesion is both the level of unity within the group and the ability to act as a unit to get the job done. Cohesion can be built up over time through the shared experiences of working together towards a common goal. It is further strengthened when the team likes and values each other and offers a sense of belonging which reinforces to each person that they are where they should be. Details matter little when the members of your tribe understand why they are they, why they have been chosen and what their overall mission is. That's what brings a team together or tears them apart – how in sync their value systems are.

A major challenge to any team's unity is when the value systems reveal themselves to be different than imagined. A classic example of this is work ethic. Work ethic is one of those things that you either have, or you do not. Sometimes work ethic can be instilled and shown to be valuable to those that do not have it. Look at the word, ethic for a moment. An ethic is a principle you believe to be true and inherently valuable. It's usually just one piece of many that contributes to how you see the world.

Work ethic is the idea that you inherently value and respect a job well done and expect others to earn their keep. People who share this mindset and attitude about work have little patience for those who take it easy and care little for the job's outcome. These two camps will always be at odds, and it should be clear that not everyone is suited to every job.

When it comes time for the division of labor you should consider the abilities and also the value systems of those that work for you. Put the aces in their places. Those who like to work should be in the roles that work for them, and those who do not like work should either be promoted to customer or reassigned to a role that will suit them.

The Servant Leader

No matter what job you find yourself in, people are always going to be your greatest resource, how you treat them and lead them will directly impact your ability to lead them. There are two types of customer – internal and external. Employees are your internal customer. Your internal customers need to be supported and served first if they are to build a relationship with your external customers. Embrace a service mindset to build a relationship with both types of customers.

It cannot be stated enough; the people that work for you are your single greatest asset. Mismanaging such an important edge could prove to be a disaster financially for any company or leader who fails to really understand this simple fact. Really take the time to consider how important it is that your people are well cared for and supported so that they can continue to be your most competitive edge.

Understanding employees and what they want is not rocket science by any stretch. They want simple things and they expect you to deliver on those things every day. Failure to do so will see them packing for greener pastures. What do they want? In a nutshell they want to know and feel that you have their back and want to see them succeed. That's really it.

Creating a positive and fun environment where they are allowed to make mistakes and learn is a part of building a great workplace in the modern world. Managing results is not always an effective way to go, and frankly can do more harm than good. Positive results will happen when people know what is expected of them and have been setup to win. Think mentor or teacher instead of the hovering coach.

When it comes to leading others and building a relationship with them, adopt a service mindset. Your team mates are not pawns, and should not be treated as disposable. In order for others to open up to you and accept you as their leader, you need to show that you are worthy of it and someone worth following. Serving their needs by providing and supporting them at work and life will create the bridge to their best self.

Just as in any relationship with another person, if it becomes clear that one side is always taking and the other is always giving, that relationship is doomed. The side who keeps giving will figure it out eventually and move on. This is a simple reason that so many people in the world hate their boss and hate their job. They feel like that are being taken advantage of and disrespected in their interactions with their boss or company.

Customer service is vital to a company's success long term. If a company hopes to reach their customer base and build brand loyalty they need to get the customer interaction piece figured out. Not only do they have to figure it out, they need to ensure that it is executed each and every time so that each time a customer interacts with the employee, it's a positive one. Customers begin to feel and think a certain way about the brand in question based on their interactions with that company's employees. Employees are no different.

In fact, it's exactly the same concept. Employees are very much the internal customer. Building brand loyalty and a positive association to the brand should be the primary focus of any company worth their salt.

Unfortunately, very few companies see it this way. Too many companies still see their employees as objects and not as the powerful edge that they are when it comes to competing in the marketplace. Employees need to know and feel that their company has got their back. It should stand to reason that an employee who is well paid, supported, trained and motivated will build superior interactions with the customers they serve each day.

Catch Them Doing Something Right

Positive reinforcement goes a long way. Constantly nitpicking every little thing your employee did wrong will send them packing. Instead of waiting for them to screw it up, catch them in the act of doing something right. Praise their success and motivate them by illustrating in plain English what they did right today and downplay the bad.

Creating a great workplace that encourages people to give their best each day doesn't happen by accident. In fact it's all part of a well-crafted plan of attack to build up your influence based upon shared respect and contribution.

Generally, you have to believe that people want to do a good job and that they enjoy seeing a project turn out well. It can be hard at times to see the best in others and assume the best in them. You are human after all. Many leaders and companies become jaded over time and assume that their employees hate everything. This is almost always because employees are often shown no respect and treated poorly based on those negative assumptions. Companies assume that their people are lazy and not worth investing in, and in turn those employees do not feel valued or respected and withdraw. This cycle of disrespect will continue on forever if nothing is done about it. You need to be that change that breaks the cycle.

One of the biggest bones of contention for employees is how they are coached. How they feel about you and the company is based on how you treat them. If you show no respect to them, it's only natural they will show you no respect either. Inexperienced leaders tend to over coach and dominate work situations because they do not feel secure in their position. Some leaders who have taken on a negative outlook on their employees will tend to over manage all aspects of their workday because they don't trust them to deliver. Lastly, there are those managers who will over coach their team in order to aggressively display their undeniable worth. Often all of these examples are true and are happening all at once, forcing leadership teams into frenzies to appear to their superiors that they are in the driver's seat. Unfortunately, all of this nonsense doesn't translate well to the employees who generally want to be left alone.

The best way to coach your team is to catch them doing something right, as opposed to something wrong. The stress of your boss looking over your shoulder waiting for you to mess up is plain counterproductive. This is true for you as the boss and for your team especially. Highlight what they have done right, and do it publicly. Make it a point to praise your team for helping you achieve this or that. When it comes time to share the good or bad results, keep it positive and keep it light. Remember, they can't possibly care on the same level as you, at least not yet.

If you are constantly posturing and ensuring that your team is reminded you are in charge, you aren't really in charge, then. Drop the games, drop the posturing and take up the mantle of teacher and mentor instead. Let your employees know what's expected of them and allow them to figure it out.

Showcase the good they are doing and tie it back in to your plan for the store/company. Put a positive spin on bad events and trivialize what is indeed trivial. When it does come to make a point about something that is actually bad, people will stand up and take notice.

Conclusion: Wrap Up and Next Steps

If you have read this far, dear reader – THANK YOU !

I have been so lucky and fortunate to have readers and supporters (like you!) that continue to inspire me each day to keep on writing! If you enjoyed this book, please consider sharing it with a friend, co-worker or family member that would enjoy it too. Thanks!

There are tons of people out there who think and feel about the world as we do. So my ask that if you enjoyed this book, please consider giving me a great star rating on the Amazon Kindle Store and of course leaving a nice comment! Not only will it help me out, it will help others who see the world as we do to find this book too.

You can also head on over to my site https://jarrodsblog.com/ for more books, articles and helpful tidbits of information to help you reach your full potential.

That's all for now and thanks again for reading my book. I hope you enjoyed it as much as I did making it. Talk soon!

- Jarrod W. Allen

www.ingramcontent.com/pod-product-compliance
Lightning Source LLC
Chambersburg PA
CBHW051219170526
45166CB00005B/1966